EXPLORATION AND EXPLOSION

T0062032

COLUMBIA SPACE SHUTTLE DISASTER

Virginia Loh-Hagan

45TH PARALLEL PRESS

Published in the United States of America by Cherry Lake Publishing
Ann Arbor, Michigan
www.cherrylakepublishing.com

Reading Adviser: Beth Walker Gambro, MS, Ed., Reading Consultant, Yorkville, IL
Cover Designer: Felicia Macheske

Photo Credits: © 19 STUDIO/Shutterstock.com, cover, 1; © Dima Zel/Shutterstock.com, 5; © Tomasz Szymanski/
Shutterstock.com, 6; © sripfoto/Shutterstock.com, 9; © Orhan Cam/Shutterstock.com, 11; © 0300309/ NASA, 12;
© LEE SNIDER PHOTO IMAGES/Shutterstock.com, 13; © KSC-03pd1016/NASA, 17; © Alan Freed/Shutterstock.com, 18;
© Sandro Pavlov/Shutterstock.com, 21; © Matej Pavlansky/Shutterstock.com, 22; © Supamotion/Shutterstock.com, 25;
© sdecoret/Shutterstock.com, 29

Graphic Elements Throughout: © Chipmunk131/Shutterstock.com; © Nowik Sylwia/Shutterstock.com;
© Andrey_Popov/Shutterstock.com; © NadzeyaShanchuk/Shutterstock.com; © KathyGold/Shutterstock.com;
© Black creator/Shutterstock.com; © Edvard Molnar/Shutterstock.com; © Elenadesign/Shutterstock.com;
© estherpoon/Shutterstock.com

45th Parallel Press is an imprint of Cherry Lake Publishing.

Library of Congress Cataloging-in-Publication Data
Names: Loh-Hagan, Virginia, author.
Title: Exploration and explosion: Columbia space shuttle disaster/ by Virginia Loh-Hagan.
Description: Ann Arbor, Michigan : Cherry Lake Publishing, [2022] | Series: Behind the curtain | Includes
    bibliographical references.
Identifiers: LCCN 2021037481 | ISBN 9781534199453 (hardcover) | ISBN 9781668900598 (paperback) |
    ISBN 9781668902035 (pdf) | ISBN 9781668906354 (ebook)
Subjects: LCSH: Columbia (Spacecraft)—Accidents—Juvenile literature. | Astronautics—United States—Juvenile
    literature. | Outer space—Exploration—Juvenile literature. | Manned space flight—Juvenile literature.
Classification: LCC TL867 .L643 2022 | DDC 629.45—dc23
LC record available at https://lccn.loc.gov/2021037481

Cherry Lake Publishing would like to acknowledge the work of the Partnership for 21st Century Learning,
a Network of Battelle for Kids. Please visit *http://www.battelleforkids.org/networks/p21* for more information.

Printed in the United States of America
Corporate Graphics

A Note on Dramatic Retellings

Participating in Readers Theater, or dramatic retellings, can greatly improve reading skills, especially fluency. The books in the **BEHIND THE CURTAIN** series give readers opportunities to learn about important historical events in a fun and engaging way. These books serve as a bridge to more complex texts. All the characters and stories have been fictionalized. To learn more, check out the Perspectives Library series and the Modern Perspectives series, as **BEHIND THE CURTAIN** books are aligned to these stories.

TABLE of CONTENTS

HISTORICAL
BACKGROUND

Humans have always wondered about space. In 1957, the Soviet Union launched the satellite *Sputnik I*. It orbited Earth. This started the race to space. In 1958, the National Aeronautics and Space Administration (NASA) was created to lead the U.S. space program.

In 1961, Alan Shepard became the first American to fly into space. In 1962, John Glenn became the first American to orbit Earth. In 1969, Neil Armstrong became the first person to walk on the Moon.

The United States has launched several space objects. It has launched several missions. It helped build the International Space Station (ISS).

FLASH FACT!

The International Space Station is a research lab. It has been visited by people from 19 countries.

Vocabulary

satellite (SA-tuh-lyte) a space object that orbits around a planet to collect information or for communication

Vocabulary

tragedies (TRA-juh-deez) events causing great suffering

liftoff (LIFT-off) the action of an aircraft becoming airborne

civilian (suh-VIL-yuhn) a person not in the armed forces

atmosphere (AT-muh-sfihr) the envelope of gases surrounding Earth

There's much to celebrate. There are also tragedies. The *Challenger* was a space shuttle. In 1986, it blew up at liftoff. All 7 crew members died. Christa McAuliffe was a teacher. She was one of the crew members. She would have been the first civilian in space.

Columbia was a space shuttle. It was the first shuttle to fly in space. Its first flight was in 1981. It completed 27 missions. In 2003, it exploded. This was the second shuttle explosion. *Columbia* was in space for 16 days. It was scheduled to return to Earth. It broke apart while entering Earth's atmosphere. All 7 crew members died.

CAST of CHARACTERS

NARRATOR: person who helps tells the story

ROSARIO: a news reporter and the mother of Tanya and Rufus

TANYA: a young girl who wants to be an astronaut; Rufus's sister

RUFUS: a young boy; Tanya's brother

MATT: the father of Tanya and Rufus who is in the armed forces

SPOTLIGHT

AMPLIFICATION OF AN ACTIVIST

Elon Musk is a business owner. He believes in solar energy and sustainability. Sustainability means carefully using resources. He wants to ensure "civilization can continue to progress." He owns Tesla. This company makes electric cars and solar panels. His other company is SpaceX. SpaceX is a private spaceflight company. It sends supplies to the International Space Station. It's building powerful rockets. It's building spacecraft to carry people into space. Musk wants to create a colony on Mars. He believes Mars colonization is humans' long-term survival plan. Traveling to Mars is dangerous. Musk said, "It's uncomfortable. It's a long journey. You might not come back alive." But Musk is still willing to go. He said, "I would like to die on Mars. Just not on impact."

FLASH FACT!

The Outer Space Treaty of 1967 states that all area in space "belongs to mankind." Space cannot be claimed by any country on Earth.

NARRATOR: *It's February 1, 2003. Columbia exploded. It's nighttime.* **ROSARIO** *gets home after work.* **TANYA** *and* **RUFUS** *are watching TV. They live in Dallas, Texas.*

ROSARIO: It's been a long day at work. Sorry about coming home late.

TANYA: We understand. We saw you reporting the news on TV.

ROSARIO: So you know about the explosion?

TANYA: Yes. It's so sad. We felt the house shake.

RUFUS: We ran outside.

TANYA: We saw a bright dot. The dot raced across the sky. It turned into streaks of smoke. These streaks were coming down from the sky

RUFUS: Then we heard a loud, rolling boom.

TANYA: What happened?

ROSARIO: *Columbia* exploded during **reentry**. At that time, it was flying at 18 times the speed of sound.

Vocabulary
reentry (ree-EN-tree)
the process of returning from outer space to Earth's atmosphere

FLASH FACT!

There's a Columbia memorial at Arlington National Cemetery in Virginia. It has an outline of a shuttle.

RUFUS: That's really fast. How high was it?

ROSARIO: It was about 201,000 feet (61,265 meters) above Dallas. It was supposed to land at Kennedy Space Center in Florida.

TANYA: Why did it explode?

ROSARIO: NASA scientists are still trying to figure out what happened. They're working hard. They're sending out search teams.

RUFUS: What happened to the astronauts?

ROSARIO: They all died. They gave their lives for science.

TANYA: What were they doing in space?

ROSARIO: The crew was on a research mission. They did more than 80 science experiments. They worked 24 hours a day in 2 shifts.

TANYA: They were heroes. But it's still a terrible loss.

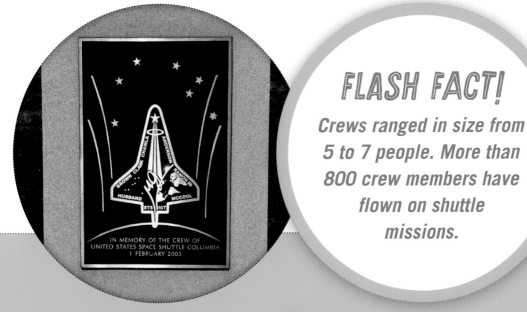

FLASH FACT!

Crews ranged in size from 5 to 7 people. More than 800 crew members have flown on shuttle missions.

NARRATOR: *Several weeks have passed. Tanya, Rosario, and Rufus are at home. They're eating dinner.*

TANYA: Have you heard any more news about the space shuttle? Do you know why it exploded?

ROSARIO: We just got the NASA reports. I reported on it today.

RUFUS: What happened?

ROSARIO: A piece of foam fell off the shuttle's **external** fuel tank. It hit the shuttle's left wing. It punched a hole and cracked some of the wing's **heat-resistant** tiles. This happened 82 seconds after liftoff.

TANYA: Wait a minute. That was 16 days before the explosion.

ROSARIO: That's right. NASA knew what happened. But they didn't know how bad the damage was.

SPOTLIGHT
A SPECIAL EFFECT

Roundworms survived the *Columbia* explosion. The astronauts were doing a study on them. They put the roundworms in a metal container. Somehow, the worms survived the intense heat and the explosion. They suffered some heat damage on the outside, but they were basically fine. The metal container helped saved them. It was placed in a special locker. It was in a part of the shuttle. This part fell. Upon impact, it slowed down. The roundworms landed more gently. Scientists learned more about life-forms in space from the worms. They learned about how space affects bodies. Descendants of the *Columbia* roundworms are at the University of Minnesota. They're being studied there. Some of the descendants flew in space. They were on the *Endeavor* shuttle in 2011.

Vocabulary
external (ek-STUHR-nuhl) belonging to or forming on the outer surface
heat-resistant (HEET-rih-ZIH-stuhnt) not easily burned or melted

FLASH FACT!
The external tank provides fuel to the shuttle's main engines during launch.

TANYA: What happened at reentry?

ROSARIO: The shuttle couldn't take the extreme heat.

RUFUS: Is it because of the hole? Did the hole damage the shuttle?

ROSARIO: Yes. Super-hot gases entered the hole. This caused the wing to fail. The shuttle lost control. It exploded into pieces.

TANYA: How did NASA figure this out?

ROSARIO: Experts studied what was left of the shuttle. **Debris** dropped from the sky. Pieces were found in more than 2,000 different places. They were found in Texas, Arkansas, and Louisiana.

TANYA: Were they able to find all the pieces?

ROSARIO: Only 40 percent have been found. Some pieces burned up. Some may never be found.

Vocabulary
debris (duh-BREE)
the remains of something broken down or destroyed

FLASH FACT!
After the explosion, NASA stopped space travel for more than 2 years. They investigated what happened.

TANYA: The news said 2 pilots died too. Is that true?

ROSARIO: Yes. Two pilots were on a helicopter. They were searching for the **wreckage**. Their helicopter lost power and crashed. They died, and 3 other people were hurt.

RUFUS: I feel so bad for their families.

ROSARIO: The pilots gave their lives for science too. Because of their work, we can learn what happened. We can make sure this doesn't happen again.

TANYA: What can the scientists do?

ROSARIO: They'll learn to build better shuttles. They'll **upgrade** the tanks. Astronauts can do more **inspections** in space. They can check heat shields. They can do this before they land.

TANYA: We have to keep learning.

Vocabulary

wreckage (REH-kij) the remains of something that has been badly damaged or destroyed

upgrade (UHP-grayd) improve

inspections (in-SPEK-shuhnz) checks to make sure something is operating properly

FLASH FACT!

Space shuttles are designed to last at least 100 missions. New technology is needed.

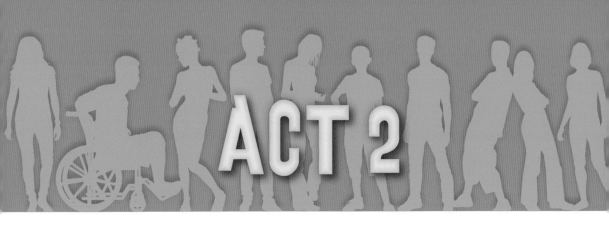

ACT 2

NARRATOR: *It is 10 years later.* **MATT** *is the father of* **TANYA** *and* **RUFUS**. *Tanya and Rufus are in college. They're home for winter break. Matt, Tanya, and Rufus are talking.*

MATT: Are you sure you want to be an astronaut?

TANYA: Yes. I researched what I need to do. I'm working on a computer science degree. I'm signing up for flying lessons. I'm working out every day. I need to pass a **physical**.

RUFUS: The *Columbia* explosion didn't scare you?

TANYA: No. It inspired me. Those astronauts did amazing work in space. I want to discover new worlds. I want to work with high-tech tools.

RUFUS: You just want to wear the space suit.

TANYA: That's definitely true too. That suit is pretty cool!

MATT: Remember all the people who died? Are you willing to risk your life? Space travel is dangerous.

Vocabulary

physical (FIH-zuh-kuhl) doctor's examination that measures a person's fitness

FLASH FACT!

Astronaut trainees have to pass tough swim tests. They spend a lot of time underwater.

Vocabulary
robotic (roh-BAH-tik)
made of machines

FLASH FACT!

Space technology has inspired many inventions. These inventions are used on Earth. They're called NASA spinoffs. Examples are memory foam, LED lighting, and GPS.

TANYA: It's hard to think about. But the danger is worth it to me.

MATT: I think it's all a waste of money. Billions of dollars are spent on the space program. That's my tax money. I don't see any benefits.

TANYA: There are many benefits. Space missions have developed important technology. **Robotic** arms used in surgery are an example. Cordless vacuum cleaners are another. We wouldn't have these tools without the space program.

MATT: I still don't see it.

TANYA: Dad, you're in the military. Satellites help you. Without them, you'd lose wars.

MATT: How so?

TANYA: Satellites give us information. They provide information about enemy movements to the military. They give early warnings of missile attacks. They also provide **navigation**. They give information about weather.

MATT: I'm still not convinced. There are other ways to spend our tax money.

TANYA: Another reason for space travel is to explore planets. One day, we might need another planet to live on. We have to find one that allows human survival.

MATT: Who wants to live on Mars? That's silly.

Vocabulary

navigation (na-vuh-GAY-shuhn) the process of getting from place to place

global warming (GLOH-buhl WAHRM-ing) the long-term heating of Earth's climate due to human activities

FLASH FACT!

About 110 people would be needed to colonize Mars. It would take 7 months to travel to Mars.

RUFUS: I don't know about that. It seems like it could be a reality. I read some science reports about it. Colonizing Mars could happen.

MATT: That'll only happen in movies.

TANYA: Think about **global warming**. We are destroying our planet. Mars may be our only option.

RUFUS: We'll just end up trashing Mars. Look at all the space junk floating around.

MATT: There's space junk?

RUFUS: Every time we go to space, debris gets left behind. Hundreds of thousands of human-made objects are in orbit.

MATT: What's up there?

RUFUS: There are pieces of satellites. There are pieces of spacecraft. There are even paint chips.

MATT: It sounds like humans are the problem. Even if we go to Mars, we'll still have problems.

RUFUS: Maybe Dad has a point. We should be spending money to fix Earth instead.

MATT: We could feed hungry people.

RUFUSU: We could house the homeless.

MATT: We could fix **climate change**. That's another idea! Why don't you become a climate scientist? That would be more useful!

TANYA: As an astronaut, I would be studying space climate.

SPOTLIGHT
EXTRA! EXTRA! BONUS FACT!

Sir Richard Branson is an English business owner. He owns many companies. For example, he owns Virgin Atlantic Airways. In 2004, he started Virgin Galactic. This is a spaceflight company for space tourists. In 2021, Branson traveled to space. He traveled on a Virgin Galactic spacecraft called VSS *Unity*. He became the first billionaire founder of a space company to travel to the edge of space. He also became the first to ride his own spacecraft. His mission lasted about 1 hour. It took him 17 years to get this spaceflight ready. Branson said, "I have dreamt of this moment since I was a kid but honestly, nothing could prepare you for the view of Earth from space." He's selling tickets to space. It's expensive. A ticket for the 1-hour trip is $450,000. The cost includes training and a spacesuit.

Vocabulary
climate change (KLY-muht CHAYNJ) a change in the usual weather in a place, often caused by global warming

FLASH FACT!
Scientists want to turn space junk into fuel.

MATT: Space travel is really hard on human bodies.

RUFUS: Being in **zero gravity** is no joke.

TANYA: It can make bones **brittle**. It can weaken muscles.

MATT: Doesn't this scare you?

TANYA: Of course, I'm scared. It's outer space!

RUFUS: Don't forget the dangerous aliens.

TANYA: Why do we think aliens are dangerous? The movies make aliens out to be scary. But they could be like us.

MATT: Aliens aren't real.

TANYA: I don't know about that. We need to do more research. That's what I want to do. I want to see what's out there.

MATT: There's so much on Earth you could explore. About 95 percent of the world's oceans have never been explored. You could be an **oceanographer**.

RUFUS: There are dangers with ocean science as well.

TANYA: I know the risks of space travel. But the rewards are worth it. Exploring space is exciting. We've learned so much. But there's so much more to learn.

Vocabulary

zero gravity
(ZIR-oh GRA-vuh-tee) state of being weightless

brittle (BRIH-tuhl)
thin and easily breakable

oceanographer
(oh-shuh-NAH-gruh-fuhr)
a person who studies the ocean

FLASH FACT!
SETI is the Search for Extraterrestrial Intelligence. The SETI Institute studies life-forms in the universe.

FLASH FORWARD
CURRENT CONNECTIONS

The Columbia space shuttle explosion happened in 2003. But its legacy lives on. We are still feeling its effects. There is still so much work for us to do.

- **Honor those who died:** Visit the "Forever Remembered" exhibit. The Kennedy Space Center opened this special exhibit in 2015. The Center displayed debris from both the *Challenger* and *Columbia* missions. This was the first time NASA did something like this. The exhibit has the *Challenger*'s main body. It has the *Columbia*'s window frames. It also has personal things from the 14 astronauts who died. The Center worked with the astronauts' families. It's important to remember those who sacrificed their lives.

- **Learn pros and cons of space tourism:** Space tourism is traveling to space for fun. Companies are working on spaceflight. These companies include Virgin Galactic and SpaceX. There are issues with space tourism. First, it's very expensive. Only rich people can afford it. Second, space tourism could affect the planet. Rockets emit soot or black carbon. This soot can't be washed away. It could cause climate change. It's important to think about the results of our actions.

- **Take care of our universe:** More activities are taking place in space. There are spaceflights. There are satellite mega-constellations. These are networks of thousands of satellites in space. All space activity leaves behind debris. Some debris burns up. But some orbits Earth. More space trash means more chances of crashes. This could make space travel even more dangerous.

CONSIDER THIS!

TAKE A POSITION! Research how much money is spent on space programs. Some people think space programs are needed for national security. Some think they're needed for science. Do you think space programs are worth the money? Argue your point with reasons and evidence.

SAY WHAT? Learn about how space affects human bodies. Explain these effects. Describe what happens.

THINK ABOUT IT! Learn more about Mars colonization. Learn the pros and cons. Would you be willing to live on Mars? Think about your skills. Why would you be a good colonist? Why would you be a bad colonist?

Learn More

Loh-Hagan, Virginia. *Lost in Space Hacks.* Ann Arbor, MI: Cherry Lake Publishing, 2019.

Loh-Hagan, Virginia. *Mars Colonization.* Ann Arbor, MI: Cherry Lake Publishing, 2020.

Loh-Hagan, Virginia. *Weird Science: Space.* Ann Arbor, MI: Cherry Lake Publishing, 2021.

Orr, Tamra B. *Columbia Space Shuttle Explosion and Space Exploration.* Ann Arbor, MI: Cherry Lake Publishing, 2018.

INDEX

ABOUT THE AUTHOR

Dr. Virginia Loh-Hagan is an author, former K–8 teacher, curriculum designer, and university professor. She's currently the director of the Asian Pacific Islander Desi American (APIDA) Center at San Diego State University. She has Tesla solar panels. That's as close to outer space as she cares to be. She lives in San Diego with her one very tall husband and two very naughty dogs.